S0-FQO-652

The Satisfying Presence of God:

The Satisfying Presence of God:
Devotions for Guatemala 2019

Kevin R. Burgess

Cover designed by Emily Sirota

2018

Copyright © 2018 by Kevin R. Burgess
ISBN #: 978-0-359-15356-5

All rights reserved. This book or any portion thereof may not be reproduced or used in any manner whatsoever without the express written permission of the publisher except for the use of brief quotations in a book review or scholarly journal.

First Printing: 2018

Unless otherwise indicated, all scripture quotations are from the ESV® Bible (The Holy Bible, English Standard Version®), copyright © 2001 by Crossway, a publishing ministry of Good News Publishers. Used by permission. All rights reserved.

Scripture noted as NASB taken from the NEW AMERICAN STANDARD BIBLE®, Copyright © 1960, 1962, 1963, 1968, 1971, 1972, 1973, 1975, 1977, 1995 by The Lockman Foundation. Used by permission.

Contact email: keviburg@gmail.com

Dedication

To the 2019 New Year's mission team to Guatemala

Without you, this devotional wouldn't exist. It is the culmination of prayer and study leading me to "*gaze upon the beauty of His presence*" (Psalm 27:4) and gain a glimpse into the eyes of our Lord.

There will be many opportunities on this trip to "*be still and know that I am God*" (Psalm 46:10 KJV). There will rarely be internet access or television, so we have an incredible opportunity to spend time meditating on the living and piercing Word of God.

May His Spirit arrest your soul and lead you into His sweet, satisfying presence.

Acknowledgements

I would like to thank Emily Sirota for her exquisite artwork on the cover. Emily, you quickly grasped the vision of this devotional and made it come to life. You readily accepted the challenge and were the perfect person to do the artwork.

Thank you for pouring you heart and soul into this project. You are a treasure!

Contents

Seeking His Presence in Guatemala (Dec 27, 2018)

"Is it not in your going with us, so that we are distinct, I and your people, from every other people on the face of the earth?" Ex 33:16

Some of the most sweet and tender moments on our mission trip will be the time we spend together doing team devotions. The devotions are important to me and I begin seeking God's guidance long before the trip begins for just the right theme.

After last year's trip, I began studying Matthew 13:44-45, two parables about the significant value of the Kingdom of God. In verse 44, a man found treasure in a field. He sold all that he had and purchased that field to possess the treasure. In verse 45, a pearl broker found a pearl of tremendous value. He sold all that he had and bought that pearl. These parables teach of the significant value of the Kingdom of God. After all, who can put a value on the Kingdom of God? This was a great theme, but I didn't have peace about using this passage for our devotions.

After some time, I thought the devotion could be based on the armor of God described in Ephesians 6. "That would be perfect!", I thought to myself. So, I studied each piece of armor, from the belt of truth to the sword of the Spirit. As significant as this passage is in understanding the spiritual world, I did not have peace in my heart about using it for our devotions.

One day, as I was praying, it seemed the Lord was telling me to find a theme that moved me personally. In other words, to have a passion for our devotion time, the theme would need to resonate in my heart. This was an epiphany for me because, while I thought He was having me prepare these devotions for your benefit, in reality, He was softening and molding *my own* heart!

In Exodus 33:16, Moses knew the presence of God would make God's people distinct and different. In God's presence, the Israelites were able to carry out God's instructions. Likewise, being in His presence while we are in Guatemala will set us apart, make us unique, and ultimately allow us to carry out His plan for our time here.

To set the context for our study, there are a few things to keep in mind. First, God is omnipresent, which means He is present everywhere all at the same time. Not one person is physically closer to or farther from God than any other person other at any time. Psalm 139:7 says, *"Where shall I go from your Spirit? Or where shall I flee from your presence?"* When we talk about His presence, we do not mean He only exists in certain places at certain times. He is everywhere all at the same time. In this devotional, God's presence means God manifesting Himself, so His people can interact with Him.

A great example of God manifesting Himself to mentor someone is found in Genesis 4:6-7. After Cain's sacrifice was not worthy, he was *"angry and his face fell"*. God told Cain that *"sin is crouching at the door"* and *"you must rule over it"*. Cain was not able to heed God's advice and suffered significantly because of it. Cain told God in verse 13, *"My punishment is greater than I can bear"*. The point is, once you have been in His presence, He will show you things. Don't ignore these things, because God will let you make your own choices with either blessings or consequences afterward.

Second, His presence is not a feeling. Sometimes we can feel things and believe God is speaking to us, when it might only be heartburn from the change in our diet in Guatemala! We encounter His presence when we *"gaze upon the beauty of the Lord"* (Psalm 27:4) and rejoice as we see His glory and majesty. When our soul, through the Holy Spirit, looks into the eyes of Christ and we are *"strengthened with power through His Spirit in your inner being"* (Ephesians 3:16). His presence brings delight to our souls.

Our devotions will be based on Exodus 33:12-23. This is the passage where Moses asked God to show him His presence. God's response was to show him the backside of His glory, while hiding him in a rock.

Additional reading: Exodus 33:12-23

Coram Deo – Living before the face of God

Did anything from this day's devotion resonate with you?
Did God reveal something about His presence today?

_____

_____

_____

_____

_____

_____

_____

_____

_____

_____

_____

_____

_____

_____

_____

_____

_____

_____

_____

_____

Coram Deo – Living before the face of God

_____

_____

_____

_____

_____

_____

_____

_____

_____

_____

_____

_____

_____

_____

_____

_____

_____

_____

_____

_____

_____

Coram Deo – Living before the face of God

Coram Deo – Living before the face of God

_____

_____

_____

_____

_____

_____

_____

_____

_____

_____

_____

_____

_____

_____

_____

_____

_____

_____

_____

Encountering God's Presence (Dec 28, 2018)

"I will make all my goodness pass before you" v. 19

Many go through life never encountering the presence of God. They go to church, go on mission trips and work at homeless shelters, but never experience the presence of God. My prayer it that we, as a team, come to recognize God's presence; not only while we are in Guatemala, but continue seeking His presence for the rest of our lives.

It just doesn't seem fair how often Moses got the privilege to be in God's presence. Imagine this happening to you…one day you are minding your own business and notice a bush burning but not consumed. That would probably intrigue you (I know it would intrigue me)! As you turn and start to move closer, God (probably in the booming voice of James Earl Jones) boldly calls your name twice! And you respond, "Yes, it is me." Then God says, "Do not come near me. Take your shoes off, because the ground you are standing on is holy ground." You would no doubt take off our shoes because the presence of God is a holy place.

Then imagine God saying, "I am the God of Abraham, Isaac and Jacob." When this happened to Moses, he hid his face because he was afraid to look at God. This same fear would no doubt be in your heart as you come into the physical presence of God.

You might say to yourself, "But this ground is nothing special! I've walked by it every day on my way to work or school." But then you realize the ground is not inherently holy, it is holy because God is there.

To give some context, Moses was a Hebrew who was raised in the land of Egypt. He was brought up in the house of Pharaoh until he killed an Egyptian and fled from pharaoh to the land of Midian. It was at this burning bush where God told Moses to go and lead His people out of Egypt.

You have most likely seen the movie "The Ten Commandments" with Charlton Heston, so you remember all God did through Moses. Moses went from doubting his capabilities to becoming a vessel used to display God's glory and power. He went from feeling unworthy as a leader for his people to leading them through the divided Red Sea with the Egyptians bearing down on them. He went from his identity as a fleeing shepherd in the land of Midian to possessing the law of God.

Have you ever doubted your ability to be God's messenger? Have you ever felt overwhelmed and unworthy to carry out His plan? Spending time in His presence will change you from doubting your ability, to becoming a vessel used by God. His presence will change you from feeling unworthy, to leading others through tough times in their spiritual lives. Spending time in God's presence will change your identity, and you will become someone who carries out God's plan with boldness rather than seeking your own desires.

While God can and has manifested Himself physically after the crucifixion, that is not the way we typically encounter Him today. He has given us His Spirit who lives inside us. In Romans 8:16, The Apostle Paul said, "The Spirit himself bears witness with our spirit that we are children of God". Today, we encounter Him spiritually. John MacArthur said it well, "God the Father called in the Old Testament, God the Son called in the New Testament and God the Holy Spirit is calling today. And the call of the Holy Spirit today come from the compulsion of the heart."

On a mission trip to Romania many years ago, our team gave Romanian New Testaments to a crowd that had gathered around us. I am embarrassed to say I had one in my pocket that I was wanting to save. I didn't know why I was saving it, and we had run out completely except for the one in my pocket. As we were packing the equipment, a handicapped elderly lady came up to me. Her handicap caused her to wait for the crowd to clear before she came to talk with the team. She had tears in her eyes and wanted a bible to know more about Jesus. I pulled the New Testament from my pocket and her face lit up. She gave me a big hug and a wet kiss on my cheek. God knew why He wanted me to save that one bible. The lesson I learned from this was God's presence always glorifies Himself and causes me to be more Christ-like.

Additional reading: Luke 24:13-25

Coram Deo – Living before the face of God

Did anything from this day's devotion resonate with you?
Did God reveal something about His presence today?

_____

_____

_____

_____

_____

_____

_____

_____

_____

_____

_____

_____

_____

_____

_____

_____

_____

_____

_____

Coram Deo – Living before the face of God

Coram Deo – Living before the face of God

Coram Deo – Living before the face of God

His Presence is Possible (Dec 29, 2018)

"My presence will go with you" v. 14

"There has to be more to the Christian life than this!" exclaimed a friend who had recently lost the love of his life. "There must be more to the Christian life than simply existing on this earth and going to heaven when we die! He was searching for meaning in his Christian life, amid tremendous pain. If you've ever lost a close friend or relative, you understand the loneliness, void and emptiness. Is there more to the Christian life than merely existing, or even worse, struggling to live a Godly life? Yes, Psalm 16:11 says, "You will make known to me the path of life; in your presence is fullness of joy; in your right hand there are pleasures forever."

It's important to understand the events that occurred prior to Moses asking for God's presence in the Exodus passage. Moses and Joshua had gone to the top of Mt. Sinai to meet with God. Moses met with God for forty days and forty nights. During this time, God gave him the ten commandments on the tablets of stone. The people of Israel had grown restless and didn't know what happened to Moses, so they thought it would be a good idea to create a golden calf as an idol and worship it.

God was extremely angry with Israel and even told Moses he was going to destroy them because they were a "stiff-necked people". Moses interceded for his people and God did not destroy them. After Moses and Joshua descended from the mountain and saw all the dancing and celebration to the idol, Moses became angry as well and things did not go well for the Israelites.

Moses threw the tablets at the foot of the mountain and broke them. He then took the calf and melted it. He ground it into powder, spread it over the water and made the people drink it. He requested that all those who were serious followers of God to come to him. Any who did not come to him were killed. On top of all that, God sent a plague to the Israelites as a punishment.

However, even after all this punishment, God was still extremely angry with His people. He told Moses He would send an angel to be in their presence because if He stayed in their presence, He would likely consume them, because they were a "stiff-necked people". Moses did not want to leave Mt. Sinai without the presence of God.

Before the crucifixion, examples of God's presence were "primarily" physical. After the crucifixion, His presence became "primarily" spiritual. Granted, Jesus appeared to several after His death to validate His resurrection, like when He physically appeared to the Apostle Paul on the road to Damascus. But that is not the norm. Hebrews 9:16 attributes the Holy Spirit saying, "*I will put my laws on their hearts, and write them on their minds.*"

His presence today is not *with* us, but *in* us. Jesus said in John 16:7 "*... it is to your advantage that I go away, for if I do not go away, the Helper will not come to you. **But if I go, I will send him to you.**" The only reason a believer can experience the presence of God is because Jesus sent the Holy Spirit to be in us. Jesus said in John 14:20, "*In that day you will know that I am in my Father, and you in me, **and I in you**.*" The Lord of the universe is in me!

God is always at work around us, as Henry Blackaby said in his study called "Experiencing God". But just as important, He is at work within us. And if He shows you on the inside, what He is up to on the outside, it is His invitation for you to join Him in that work. You may feel inadequate or think that He intends for someone else to carry out that work. But if He shows you His work, join Him in it.

Are there barriers to His presence? You bet there are. God is jealous! God was threatening to leave the presence of the people of Israel because they started worshipping a golden calf! We might argue that we have never worshipped a golden calf. What about when we worship our fleshly desires? Our flesh can be demanding and cause us to pursue its desires, which are contrary to God's desires for us. Pursuing the flesh builds a wall between us and the presence of God, separating us from the joy of his presence.

Ralph Waldo Emerson captured this well when he said, "What lies behind us and what lies before us are tiny matters compared to what lies within us." There is more to life than merely existing, because He lives inside all who profess Him as Lord.

Additional reading: John 14:1-24

Coram Deo – Living before the face of God

Did anything from this day's devotion resonate with you?
Did God reveal something about His presence today?

_____

_____

_____

_____

_____

_____

_____

_____

_____

_____

_____

_____

_____

_____

_____

_____

_____

_____

_____

Coram Deo – Living before the face of God

_____

_____

_____

_____

_____

_____

_____

_____

_____

_____

_____

_____

_____

_____

_____

_____

_____

_____

_____

Coram Deo – Living before the face of God

Coram Deo – Living before the face of God

_____

_____

_____

_____

_____

_____

_____

_____

_____

_____

_____

_____

_____

_____

_____

_____

_____

_____

_____

_____

_____

Asking Persistently for His Presence (Dec 30, 2018)

"...please show me now your ways, that I may know you..." v.13
"Please show me your glory." v. 18

We have a cat named "Baby". We jokingly say that Baby didn't get enough oxygen when she was born. She loves to lick things, like wooden molding and her water bowl (the outside of it, not where the water is!). Most mornings Baby will join me as I am getting ready for work. She jumps up on the bed and meows at me, persistently until I pet her. Some days I am in a hurry, but because Baby is so persistent for love and attention, I always give it to her. This is how Moses was with God that day. He kept asking persistently and God gave him want he sought. His presence!

Moses asked God in verse 13, *"please show me now your ways, that I may know you"*. Twice after Moses asked Him, God promised he would do it; *"My presence will go with you"* (v 14) and *"This very thing you have spoken, I will do"* (v 17). Even though God had promised twice to show Moses His presence, Moses still asked again please show me your glory verse 18. Moses diligently sought God's presence, not only for himself but also the people of Israel. And he was not willing to take "no" or "I'll do it later" as an answer. The result was God honored Moses' persistence and showed him a glimpse of His glory.

As a side note, notice his motive was *"that I may know you"* (v 13). If Moses had wanted God's presence in order to increase his position among the Israelites, God would have withheld His presence, but Moses motive was pure. His motive was to know the God of Abraham, Isaac and Jacob.

There is an interesting passage Luke 11. There is man who goes to the house of a friend and wants to borrow 3 loaves of bread. The kids are already asleep, and the friend does not want to get up and wake up his kids. Those of you who have had young kids know that it's not good to wake them after they have fallen asleep, because they may not fall back asleep right away. But the man was persistent! He kept knocking until the friend got up and gave him the thing he asked.

Jesus then said in Luke 11:9, *"And I tell you, ask, and it will be given to you; seek, and you will find; knock, and it will be opened to you."*. Scholars agree the verbs used in this phrase imply it should be done continuously. Keep on asking! Keep on seeking! Keep on knocking! The context for this passage is when Jesus was teaching His disciples how to pray.

If you want His presence, ask Him. Don't just ask him once, but over and over. It is how God knows you really want to see Him. It is also how you can know you really want to see Him.

God is not an impersonal cosmic being who has no desire to commune with us. He has personality and as a personality, God thinks, wills, enjoys, feels, loves and desires. Since we were made in His image, we also have personality. One of the most rewarding things is getting to know other people. We love when others care about us, think about us and pray for us. It is because we were made in His image that we have the capability to know God. But do we have the desire in our hearts? Are we willing to diligently seek Him? He wants to interact with us and will continue to show us His presence, if we ask persistently.

In our busy lifestyles, we tend to miss Him in the midst of 'doing" good things like studying the bible, attending church services, Sunday schools and bible studies. We are busy trying to do things we believe are good, while we struggle having a relationship with God.

Since God is a personality, we can't build a relationship with Him in merely one encounter. In John 17:3 Jesus tells us, *"This is eternal life, that they know you, the only true God, and Jesus Christ whom you have sent."* The focus of our lives is to "know Him". This relationship is the reason we exist!

In Jeremiah 29:13, the prophet Jeremiah said, *"You will seek me and find me, when you seek me with all your heart."* God wants a relationship. He wants us to actively seek Him, not merely seek the ways he interacts with this world, but to seek Him.

Tozer said, 'Come near to the holy men and women of the past and you will soon feel the heat of their desire after God". It is a desire for Him that fuels a relationship where we persistently ask, seek and knock.

Additional scripture: Luke 11:1-13

Coram Deo – Living before the face of God

Did anything from this day's devotion resonate with you?
Did God reveal something about His presence today?

_____

_____

_____

_____

_____

_____

_____

_____

_____

_____

_____

_____

_____

_____

_____

_____

_____

_____

Coram Deo – Living before the face of God

Coram Deo – Living before the face of God

_____

_____

_____

_____

_____

_____

_____

_____

_____

_____

_____

_____

_____

_____

_____

_____

_____

_____

_____

_____

_____

Coram Deo – Living before the face of God

Finding Rest in God's Presence (Dec 31, 2018)

"My presence will go with you, and I will give you rest." v. 14

The first day on a mission trip to Guatemala can be extremely stressful. Team members get up very early (and probably don't sleep well the night before), get their heavy bags loaded, travel to the airport, go through security (ugh!), board their flight, arrive in Guatemala (making sure all the team members are present), go through customs, load themselves and their bags in vans, have lunch, purchase supplies for ministry, drive to James Project, have dinner, have a welcome time with the kids, and have devotions. Whew! By the end of the first day, I am exhausted! I just want to crawl in the bed, because I need...rest. It feels so good to fall asleep and recharge physically for the next day.

God told Moses one of the benefits of His presence is He would give them rest. The Israelites had been camped at Mt. Sinai for a while and they were ready to move on. God was not saying to Moses that He was going to give them physical rest, but spiritual rest.

To get a deeper meaning of finding spiritual rest in God's presence, let's take a look at a passage in Matthew 11 where Jesus said, *"Come to me, all who labor and are heavy laden, and I will give you rest. Take my yoke upon you, and learn from me, for I am gentle and lowly in heart, and you will find rest for your souls."* In the original language the term "heavy laden" refers to being over-loaded, like an animal with too much weight packed on them. They have so much weight on them that they can't walk the terrain and may collapse under it. The meaning of the word "rest" describes refreshment. When we are over-burdened with the cares of this world, we need spiritual rest. Jesus was basically saying, in Him we will find refreshment for our souls. There is no better refreshment than being in His presence.

Our souls are refreshed when we are saved, and we can go back time and time again into the presence of Christ for refreshment. Peter said in Acts 3:19, *"Therefore repent and return, so that your sins may be wiped away, in order that times of refreshing may come from the presence of the Lord*". When we are in His presence and see Him in all His majesty, it changes our perspective on our problems. An illustration of this is comparing the size of the sun with the size of a quarter. Obviously, the sun is millions of times larger than a quarter. However, if you take that quarter and put it right in front of your eye, all you see is the quarter. By moving the quarter further out, the quarter becomes small compared to the brilliance of the sun. By moving your burdens out, they become small compared to the glory of the Son. And as a bonus, He promises to also carry those burdens for you.

Do you struggle with loneliness? I don't mean being alone, but loneliness. Loneliness is defined as "sadness because one has no friends or company". A recent report indicates nearly half of the people studied say they sometimes or always feel lonely. Entering His presence gives rest from the burden of loneliness. He understands your need for a close friend. Proverbs 18:24 says it like this, "*A man of many companions may come to ruin, but there is a friend who sticks closer than a brother.*" In the presence of Christ, we can be alone but never lonely.

Our family has gone through a lot this past year. After last years' trip, I ended up in the hospital with some heart issues. I didn't know I would encounter two more emergency room visits and two more hospital stays by April. On top of that, Lisa's sister, Carol Ann, passed away in February after a valiant battle with cancer. We loved her so much. At the end of April, we needed spiritual rest. God placed this devotional on my heart and this study has refreshed my soul.

As I was wrestling with the devotion for the Guatemala trip, I began to ask God for His insight. After a prolonged struggle, His Word started coming alive to me. When I would read a passage and understand it's meaning, it was as if my soul was being satisfied. As a result, Lisa and I have decided to go to graduate school pursuing a master's degree in Biblical studies. We are not sure where this will ultimately lead, but we are trusting His plan for us. I am learning that God doesn't show me the big picture because I am to follow the next step He shows me, by faith. I am to obey Him because I love and fear Him, not because I approve of His plan.

Additional reading: Matthew 11:25-30

Coram Deo – Living before the face of God

Did anything from this day's devotion resonate with you?
Did God reveal something about His presence today?

_____

_____

_____

_____

_____

_____

_____

_____

_____

_____

_____

_____

_____

_____

_____

_____

Coram Deo – Living before the face of God

Coram Deo – Living before the face of God

Coram Deo – Living before the face of God

Preparing to be in His Presence (Jan 1, 2019)

"if I have found favor in your sight, please show me now your ways"
v.13

God has chosen throughout history to be present with His people. It is important to recognize that God is not obligated to reveal Himself. In Exodus 33:19, God said *"And I will be gracious to whom I will be gracious, and will show mercy on whom I will show mercy."* The Apostle Paul repeats this in Romans 9 and adds in verse 16 *"So then it depends not on human will or exertion, but on God who has mercy."*

Our Lord said, *"No one can come to Me unless the Father who sent Me draws him; and I will raise him up on the last day"* (John 6:44). The desire that resides in us to love Him originates in the Almighty. Even our faith comes from Him, *"For by grace you have been saved through faith. And this is not your own doing; it is the gift of God, not a result of works, so that no one may boast."* (Ephesians 2:8-9). He is the source of our spiritual lives and we owe everything to Him.

God was extremely angry with the Israelites because of their incident with the golden calf. He told Moses He would send an angel to go along with them, otherwise He might consume them. Moses knew the Israelites needed God's presence, so he pleaded with God to go with them. The main argument Moses made for God's presence with them is that he had found favor in the sight of God. You might ask "How do I find favor with God?" The answer is, *you* can't. Since the fall of Adam, we are all separated from God. Paul says in Romans 3:23, "for all have sinned and fall short of the glory of God." And it gets worse, because he then tells us in Romans 6:23 "For the wages of sin is death…" God has the right to destroy us all. We have all sinned against Him.

I am glad the story doesn't end there. The remainder of verse 23 say *"but the free gift of God is eternal life in Christ Jesus our Lord"*. If we had to depend on our own abilities, we would be eternally punished, but God has made a way for us, through His Son, Jesus Christ.

An important takeaway from the tabernacle and its laws, is the presence of God is to be taken seriously. It is a privilege to be allowed into His presence. In His presence He illuminates things about us and about His work in this world that we otherwise would not see.

Step one in preparing to be in His presence is found in Romans 10:9, *"...confess with your mouth that Jesus is Lord and believe in your heart that God raised Him from the dead, you will be saved."* God is a jealous God and will not bless His presence on anyone who does not believe in His Son.

Jesus said in John 10:9, *"I am the door; if anyone enters through Me, he will be saved, and will go in and out and find pasture"*. I love that it says, "find pasture". There is nothing more satisfying to a sheep than finding green pasture. As a sheep is satisfied when they find pasture, Christians are satisfied when encountering the presence of God.

The second step in preparing to be in His presence is to live a righteous life, dependent on the Holy Spirit. Righteous living does not save us, but it is a litmus test of our love for Christ. Jesus said in John 14:21 *"Whoever has my commandments and keeps them, he it is who loves me. And he who loves me will be loved by my Father, and I will love him and manifest myself to him."* Did you see that? Jesus said He will manifest himself to us. In other words, if we love Him, we will live a righteous life and He will manifest or disclose Himself to us! What a tremendous promise!

Living a righteous life is not easy. When we have been in His presence, we soon see that the war between the flesh and the spirit is very real. As a born-again believer, we experience two beings trapped in one fleshly body (Romans 7:22-23). On the one hand we clearly see the Spirit, who desires the things of God. On the other hand, we see the flesh, that seeks its own desires contrary to the Spirit. It is the presence of God through His Spirit that gives us the ability to walk by the Spirit and not by the flesh.

The Psalmist said in Psalm 140:13, *"Surely the righteous shall give thanks to your name; the upright shall dwell in your presence."* To dwell means to reside or live. The upright, those who live righteously, will dwell in His presence.

Additional scripture: Jeremiah 4:1-2; Psalm 90:1-17

Coram Deo – Living before the face of God

Did anything from this day's devotion resonate with you?
Did God reveal something about His presence today?

Coram Deo – Living before the face of God

Coram Deo – Living before the face of God

Coram Deo – Living before the face of God

Our Access to God's Presence (Jan 2, 2019)

"And the Lord said, Behold, there is a place by me where you shall stand on the rock" v. 21

Many people go to church expecting to see God. The interesting thing about this is that God is there, not because He resides in a building but because we bring Him with us! He resides in us! In 1 Corinthians 6:19, Paul admonishes the believers in Corinth asking, *"or do you not know that your body is a temple of the Holy Spirit within you, whom you have from God?"* God no longer resides in a physical space nor does he place special powers into objects like He did with Moses' staff. He resides in the hearts and minds of His people.

In verse 21, God told Moses to stand on the rock to experience His presence. He not only had him stand in that place, but he hid him in the cleft of the rock and protected him. God protects those in His presence. Even when others mean to harm us, God ultimately turns it into good. Joseph's brothers sold him into slavery where he went to Egypt and rose to power, went to prison and rose to power again under pharaoh. When Joseph's brothers asked forgiveness, in Genesis 50:20 Joseph said, *"you meant evil against me, but God meant it for good"*. In other words, God will sometimes use the evil of others to put us in position to serve Him.

Today we experience God's presence in our hearts and minds. To better understand this, it is important to have some background on the tabernacle. Under the old covenant, God wanted a place to be present with His people, so He gave Moses instructions on building the tabernacle. Hebrews 9:1 says the tabernacle was a model of worship under the old covenant.

In the diagram of the tabernacle below, notice there are two rooms. The larger room was called the Holy Place and contained the Table of Bread, the golden lampstand and the Altar of Incense. The smaller room included only the Ark of the Covenant, which had the mercy seat and cherubim on top of it. Separating these two rooms was a veil.

The only entrance to the Tabernacle was from the east. Access into the Holy Place was restricted. Only the Levitical priests, wearing specific clothing, could enter the Holy Place. Access through the veil

20 Gold-covered boards on the North

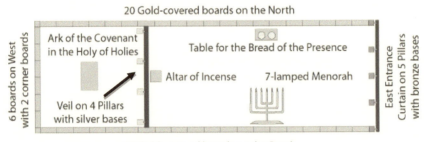

20 Gold-covered boards on the South

into the Holy of Holies, the presence of God, was further restricted. Only the High Priest could enter, and then only once per year. The reason God limited access into His presence was to demonstrate what an incredible privilege it is to be allowed in His presence. Never take it for granted!

When Jesus died on the cross, Matthew 27:51 says *"And behold, the veil of the temple was torn in two from top to bottom...NASB"* This short phrase has significant meaning to believers. The writer of Hebrews helps us understand it when He says in Hebrews 10:19-20 *"Therefore, brethren, since we have confidence to enter the holy place by the blood of Jesus, by a new and living way which He inaugurated for us through the veil, that is, His flesh...NASB"* Jesus entered into the Holy of Holies, not in the tabernacle or the temple here on earth but in heaven and provides access for us to be in the presence of God. He was the sacrifice of all sacrifices. He was and is the only one worthy to enter the presence of God on our behalf.

We now have access to the presence of God because Jesus gained access to the heavenly Holy of Holies. Does the ease and freedom of access to His presence cause us to not take it seriously? He is our High Priest and He ever lives to make intercession for us.

Additional scripture: Hebrew 9:1-10:18

Coram Deo – Living before the face of God

Did anything from this day's devotion resonate with you?
Did God reveal something about His presence today?

_____

_____

_____

_____

_____

_____

_____

_____

_____

_____

_____

_____

_____

_____

_____

_____

_____

_____

_____

Coram Deo – Living before the face of God

_____

_____

_____

_____

_____

_____

_____

_____

_____

_____

_____

_____

_____

_____

_____

_____

_____

_____

_____

_____

Coram Deo – Living before the face of God

Coram Deo – Living before the face of God

Continually Living in His Presence (Jan 3, 2019)

"Consequently, he is able to save to the uttermost those who draw near to God through him, since he always lives to make intercession for them." Hebrews 7:25

This is our last devotion together as a team on this trip. As I write this, I can't predict all that will have happened on the trip. But I know that we will have grown close as a team.

Our lives in the United States are fast-paced. Many times, we are so focused on what we need to do, who we are going to see, or how many "likes" we get on our Instagram post that we lose sight of what is happening inside of us. One of the many benefits of having been on a short-term mission trip to James Project of Latin America is, while we were busy, there were fewer distractions allowing us to see God move around us.

Manley Beasley once said, "One of our greatest challenges is to find out what God is up to, and get in on it…" We have learned that God's presence makes our lives worth living. We prepare to be in His presence by believing He is Lord and living a righteous life in response to His Lordship. By persistently asking Him to show us His presence, He is faithful and will always respond.

Spending time in His presence changes the way we look at ourselves and the world around us. When someone is bitter and hateful toward us, we will see someone who is hurting and needs a friend. When we see a person, who is different in appearance than everyone else, we will see their heart and love them regardless. We see spiritually because the Holy Spirit lives on the inside of us.

A life lived in His presence can be extremely fulfilling. The fulfillment of our relationship with Christ is based on how much we live life continually in His presence, not merely a single encounter. He "always lives to make intercession" for you. The apostle Peter said in Act 3:19-20, *"Repent therefore, and turn back, that your sins may be blotted out, that times of refreshing may come from the presence of the Lord, and that he may send the Christ appointed for you, Jesus"*. "Times of refreshing" come from being in the Lord's presence continually. A song sung by David in 1 Chronicles 16, and repeated in Psalm 105, includes the words *"Seek the Lord and his strength, seek his presence continually!"* Being in His presence continually helps us see ourselves and the world around us through His eyes. And if we see through His eyes, we will see His plan and carry it out in His power.

The bible describes the presence of God several times analogous with our sense of taste. Psalm 34:8 says *"O taste and see that the Lord is good. How blessed is the man who takes refuge in Him!"* and Hebrews 6:4-5 *"...who have tasted the heavenly gift"* and *"tasted the goodness of the word of God"*.

On a trip to China, I had the opportunity to eat a chicken's foot. Yes, a chicken's foot! Not its leg, its foot! Not wanting to offend the cook, I tried my best to eat it. But no matter how much I wanted to eat that chicken's foot, I could not get it into my mouth! I am ashamed to say that I ended up hiding it in my napkin! You know why I couldn't eat it? Because I didn't think it would taste good.

However, the word of God tastes good and satisfying for our souls. Experiencing the satisfying taste of His presence can inspire us to share our story with others, so they can to taste and see that He is good.

As we return to our busy lives, continually ask, seek and knock. Be refreshed by His presence. May the goodness of the taste of His word inspire you to share His goodness with others He has placed in your path.

There is no way to fully describe the glory of His presence. Once you have been there, you understand the joy, peace and rest that is to be found there. This is my prayer for each of you.

There is no more fitting way to end this devotional and our time together than with the words of Jude 24-25, *"Now to him who is able to keep you from stumbling and to present you blameless before the presence of his glory with great joy, to the only God, our Savior, through Jesus Christ our Lord, be glory, majesty, dominion, and authority, before all time and now and forever. Amen"*

Additional scripture: Hebrews 7:1-28

Coram Deo – Living before the face of God

Did anything from this day's devotion resonate with you?
Did God reveal something about His presence today?

_____

_____

_____

_____

_____

_____

_____

_____

_____

_____

_____

_____

_____

_____

_____

_____

_____

_____

Coram Deo – Living before the face of God

Coram Deo – Living before the face of God

Coram Deo – Living before the face of God

What Does "coram Deo" Mean?

By R.C. Sproul

This phrase literally refers to something that takes place in the presence of, or before the face of, God. To live coram Deo is to live one's entire life in the presence of God, under the authority of God, to the glory of God.

To live in the presence of God is to understand that whatever we are doing and wherever we are doing it, we are acting under the gaze of God. God is omnipresent. There is no place so remote that we can escape His penetrating gaze.

To live all of life coram Deo is to live a life of integrity. It is a life of wholeness that finds its unity and coherency in the majesty of God. A fragmented life is a life of disintegration. It is marked by inconsistency, disharmony, confusion, conflict, contradiction, and chaos.

The Christian who compartmentalizes his or her life into two sections of the religious and the nonreligious has failed to grasp the big idea. The big idea is that all of life is religious or none of life is religious. To divide life between the religious and the nonreligious is itself a sacrilege.

Integrity is found where men and women live their lives in a pattern of consistency. It is a pattern that functions the same basic way in church and out of church. It is a life that is open before God. It is a life in which all that is done is done as to the Lord. It is a life lived by principle, not expediency; by humility before God, not defiance. It is a life lived under the tutelage of conscience that is held captive by the Word of God.

Source: https://www.ligonier.org/blog/what-does-coram-deo-mean/

References

Continually seek His presence
1 Chronicles 16:11; Psalm 105:4

Trembling, quaking or terrified in His presence
Psalm 114:1 and 7; Isaiah 19:1, Isaiah 64:1-3; Job 23:15; Ezekiel 38:20

Joy, thanksgiving and singing in His presence
Psalm 16:11; Psalm 21:6; Psalm 95:2; Psalm 100:2

Christ presents you blameless before His presence
Jude 24

No human might boast in His presence
1 Corinthians 1:29

Upright dwell in His presence
Psalm 140:13

Christ entered the presence of God on our behalf
Hebrews 9:24

Detestable things are removed from His presence
Jeremiah 4:1

There is no place to flee from His presence
Psalm 139: